Cut it Out
and
Start Saving

Cut it Out
and
Start Saving

A Guide to Effectively Using Coupons and Obtaining Money from Unexpected Resources

Denise Long & Phyllis Milano

iUniverse, Inc.
New York Lincoln Shanghai

Cut it Out and Start Saving
A Guide to Effectively Using Coupons and Obtaining Money from Unexpected Resources

iUniverse books may be ordered through booksellers or by contacting:

iUniverse
2021 Pine Lake Road, Suite 100
Lincoln, NE 68512
www.iuniverse.com
1-800-Authors (1-800-288-4677)

ISBN: 978-0-595-40867-2 (pbk)
ISBN: 978-0-595-85231-4 (ebk)

Printed in the United States of America

This book is dedicated to my husband Carl for his patience, while my mother and I monopolized the computer, to my children, Scott and Nicholas for their inspiration to write this book and to Stella Michaels for believing in us

Contents

Introduction

Food sustains life, but the price of food seems to be increasing substantially. My family has found a way to keep the cost to a minimum. We even discovered ways to save on all grocery items, including meat. Let me tell you our story.

Hoping for an easier way of life than we had experienced in Long Island, New York, my family relocated to Pennsylvania. Even though the utilities cost less in Pennsylvania, housing costs rose sharply shortly after we moved here. Neither my mother nor husband could secure employment that would provide sufficient income. After evaluating our monthly expenses, it became readily apparent that the only expense we knew how to reduce was our food bill.

While living on Long Island, I began using coupons to reduce my family's food bills. I had at first stored the coupons haphazardly in a box. But when I prepared to shop, I found it difficult to locate the coupons I needed. I soon realized I needed to develop an effective system of organizing the coupons so that I could locate them easier. For more than eighteen years, I was successful in finding ways to save more than I spent. After moving to Pennsylvania, my mother and I saved a lot of money, which helped us to stretch our incomes. Four years ago, a friend joined me on one of my shopping excursions. Amazed, she asked me to teach her how to save money by using coupons. I showed her how to use the coupons effectively. She has executed this method successfully. The following is her testimonial:

To All Future Coupon Shoppers:

When it comes down to it, Denise Long is, in my opinion, the reigning rebate and coupon queen of America. Before I met Denise, my refrigerator would cry out for help. Purchasing food for a family of four can be very expensive. When I first shopped with Denise, I could not believe how little she spent ... yet her shopping cart was full. Food shopping is now an adventure rather than a chore. I look forward to shopping just to see the look on the faces of the cashiers when they see the final results.

Thanks to Denise, "Everything's free in America!" has become my catch-phrase.

Through coupons, rebates, and shopping strategies that I learned from Denise, food shopping is more like a game show. During the first year of using her techniques, I have saved a lot of money. My entire family is happier knowing that our once-barren refrigerator, pantry, and toiletry closet now contain an abundance of items. Because of her techniques, I have tried some products without cost. When I shop for my family, I often smile and triumphantly say, "Everything's free in America!"

Sincerely,
Christine "the Happy Shopper" Kline

Saving money during food shopping eventually became a game, not a chore. Each week, we verified if the percentage exceeded the previous week's savings. Over time, the food shopping ventures became easier because we knew we were getting more food for our money.

My mother and I have achieved a tremendous amount of success. We have always been concerned with helping others. This became the primary motivation for creating this book. We know we are not the only people with inadequate salaries. This book will simply explain the methods that will enable the reader to organize and store the coupons. If you want to receive e-mails for additional money-saving ideas as they become available, an e-mail address has also been provided. Furthermore, we are currently developing a seminar to help individuals and give additional information as it is acquired.

The following is an example of some of our savings. These totals do not reflect supermarket rebates or mail-in rebates from the manufacturers. Due to the length of the grocery receipts, we only copied the totals, savings, and, where available, the percentages of savings.

```
 VF        Credit                 56.43
           CHANGE                   .00
 Weis Club Savings Total........57.21
 Coupon Savings................48.90
 Your Total Savings are  65.28%106.11
   1/22/06   1:44 PM 0189 08 0014 113
```

This receipt was originally $162.54. After the club savings of $57.21 and the $48.90 in coupons were deducted, the final bill was $56.43.

```
**** TAX        .00  BAL        1.50
        Cash                    2.00
        CHANGE                   .50
Weis Club Savings Total........13.98
Coupon Savings................. 8.00
Your Total Savings are  93.61% 21.98
  2/09/06  1:32 PM 0034 04 0125 SS
```

This receipt displays an original total of $23.48. My cash layout was $1.50. The club savings was $13.98. The coupon savings was $8.00. I saved more than 93 percent.

```
        Cash                    7.00
        CHANGE                   .39
Weis Club Savings Total..... ..33.88
Coupon Savings................43.59
Your Total Savings are  78.99% 77.47
 10/23/0  1:55 AM 0189 07 0004 112
```

This receipt had an original total of $98.10, but I had three retail checks totaling $14.00 for a brand-name formula. I saved $33.88 with the club card and $43.59 with coupons. My out-of-pocket expense was $6.61. I saved 93.2 percent.

```
    TOTAL BEFORE SAVINGS    165.07
    YOUR TOTAL SAVINGS      117.50
    TOTAL AFTER SAVINGS      47.57
    TAX PAID                  1.62
****TOTAL                    49.19
    CASH                     50.00
    CHANGE                     .81

TOTAL NUMBER OF ITEMS SOLD =   39
 8/13/06  5:55 PM 0285 12 0191 162
```

The total bill was originally $165.07. Using the club card and coupons, I saved $117.50. My out-of-pocket expense was $49.19. I saved 71 percent. I bought thirty-nine items, including several brand-name products. A sample of the receipt shows the following:

- Ten pounds of bacon

- Sixteen pounds of chicken

- Four pounds of hot dogs

- Eighteen boxes of a macaroni and cheese dinner

- Five bottles of shampoo

- Five conditioners

- Two boxes of tea bags[1]

- Three cherry-flavored green teas

- Four boxes of granola bars

- Three rice pouches

The following article was printed in the March/April 2006 issue of *Refund Cents* magazine:

---

1.   Each box contained 100 tea bags, so there was a total of 200 tea bags.

A Steal of a Deal

We went on another coupon shopping spree. This $40.00 bill was reduced to $6.58 before vendor and mail-in rebates. The discounts began with a $5.00 off $40.00 coupon. The cover page of the supermarket circular had coupons for a free two-liter bottle of cola, a free one-half gallon of orange juice, a free dozen of large eggs, and one-half gallon of ice cream. Also, that week, ten items, mix or match, were on sale for $10.00. Eleven boxes of pizza rolls were obtained free with coupons. The detergent had a "try me free" offer. The glass baking dish was free after all of the offers were utilized. The cereal boxes cost $0.90 each after using the coupons. Three popular brand-name candy bars were purchased for $0.33 each. The candy bar UPC codes were mailed in for the free T-shirt offer. Most of the items were obtained at little or no cost.

Denise Long
PA

We have achieved significant savings at other places, for example, office supply stores. After all discounts were applied, I paid $0.56 for twenty-eight items by utilizing the store sales, bringing in a circular from the competitor's store, and using a coupon that the store sent to me for money off my purchase. If both stores have good sales, bring in the competitor's circular to take advantage of sales from both locations. You will not waste the gas by going to each store to get the best prices. The following is a detailed example of an extraordinary savings by using a combination of competitor circulars and coupons and buying items while they were on sale.

Item	Cost	Total purchased	Total cost
Six-pack of one-subject notebook	$0.54	Seven six-packs (forty-two notebooks)	$3.78
Folders	$0.05	Fifteen	$0.75
Crayola colored pencils	$0.25	One	$0.25
Twelve-count box of Bic pens	$0.15	Five twelve-count boxes (sixty pens)	$0.75
		Total	$5.53

Coupon	$5.00
Tax	$0.03
Total bill	$0.56

The following is the receipt from the office supply store for the items listed above:

```
1   BIC ROUNDSTIC GRIP
    070330137257                    1.48
    100% Price Guarantee  $0.15    -1.33
    Reason 01
    Form of Proof - 01
1   BIC ROUNDSTIC GRIP
    070330137264                    1.48
    100% Price Guarantee  $0.15    -1.33
    Reason 01
    Form of Proof - 01
1   BIC ROUNDSTIC GRIP
    070330137264                    1.48
    100% Price Guarantee  $0.15    -1.33
    Reason 01
    Form of Proof - 01
1   BIC ROUNDSTIC GRIP
    070330137264                    1.48
    100% Price Guarantee  $0.15    -1.33
    Reason 01
    Form of Proof - 01
1   BIC ROUNDSTIC GRIP
    070330137257                    1.48
    100% Price Guarantee  $0.15    -1.33
    Reason 01
    Form of Proof - 01
15  2-POCKET FOLDER-W/
    078767507586        0.100ea     1.50
    100% Price Guarantee  $0.05    -0.75
    Reason 01
    Form of Proof - 01
7   NOTEBOOK 1 SUB 8PK
    718103025393        0.540ea     3.78
1   CRAYOLA 12CT COLOR
    071662040123                    0.25
SUBTOTAL                            5.53
Staples Coupon NO. 8139539883318279 -5.00
    Standard Tax 6.00%              0.03
TOTAL                             $0.56

Cash                               1.00

Cash Change                        0.44
        TOTAL ITEMS    28
```

This book will explain in detail how to reduce food bills and use coupons and rebates effectively. It contains the information required to help the reader obtain similar success by properly using the manufacturer's coupons and rebates. This book will also provide information on how to use coupons for saving money on vacations, fine dining, mortgages, gifts, and donating without hurting an individual's budget and much more.

Chapter One:
Obtaining and Organizing Coupons

You can use many resources to obtain coupons. The easiest source is probably the local newspaper, particularly the weekend editions. Most weekend papers include at least one packet, and this number may increase. Always look through the magazine section. On some weeks, it may contain additional manufacturer's coupons. In some areas, an early edition is offered on Saturday. It should cost less than the traditional Sunday edition, but the main section is not included. This edition has sales circulars and the coupon section enclosed. However, not all areas or newspapers provide an early edition.

When visiting another area, purchase the weekend edition for the coupons. In both content and denomination, the coupons typically differ from each county or state. Over time, it has apparently become the common practice that Sunday papers omit the coupon section on a holiday weekend. If there is any at all, it may include a section from a specific manufacturer. After receiving the manufacturer's coupons from the weekend paper, remove the ones that your household will not use. Save them in a pile. They can be traded in coupon trains, which will be discussed later.

As an incentive, some areas may deliver a newspaper for a week to generate possible interest in new subscriptions. These papers might contain manufacturer's coupons as well as incentives from local merchants who may advertise sales. Some people receive advertisement papers at their residence for local merchants. Those papers may include valuable coupons. In our area, a local butcher offered a coupon for high-quality, low-fat meats. The price of the ground sirloin or patties was offered for $2.19 per pound. The price and quality advertised in the paper was much better than any local supermarket in our area.

Some newspapers may also give incentives when subscribers are prepaying for a yearly subscription, even if it is only for Sunday. For example, a newspaper offered in Pennsylvania gives a coupon book for discounts at several local establishments if you prepay for the one-year subscription. For example, you can:

- Buy one meal and get another meal free at many restaurants

- Buy one admission and get another admission free into local attractions

- Obtain discounts to local gyms

Unfortunately, not all newspapers offer incentives. Verify what incentives, if any, are available for receiving home delivery of the local paper.

Some people may want to know what coupons are in the newspaper to decide if there are any products that would be pertinent to their household. You can preview the coupon inserts at www.taylortownpreview.com. When considering if it is worth purchasing that week, compare the face value of the coupons that are utilized in your household to the cost of the newspaper. Even if the product is not going to be utilized that week, count it anyway. It might be necessary eventually. Some coupons are territorial to certain areas. A small portion of coupons listed on the Internet may not be included in the inserts. The face value of the coupons sometimes depends on the location. Once coupons have been obtained, clip the coupons from the inserts and other sources listed throughout this book. Cut along the dotted lines to avoid cutting the expiration dates, bar codes, or any identifying numbers. If any of the aforementioned is missing or incomplete, a merchant may not accept the coupon.

Supermarket Coupons

You can find coupons in various locations in a supermarket. They may be printed inside the box, on or under a label, or on a removable tag. Some aisles have Smart Source machines that dispense coupons. Some stores offer calendars or store magazines with coupons on groceries. Coupons are occasionally located at the pharmacy, courtesy desk, and registers. Before using coupons that were acquired from a specific store, verify they are not exclusive to that chain.

Coupon Books

Coupon books usually have a vast amount of savings. Grocery store coupons are included in some editions of the Entertainment Book, which offers discounts on a variety of things, including the following:

- Fine dining restaurants

- Retail stores

- Fast-food restaurants

- Attractions

- National offers

- Supermarkets

- Gas

- Car rentals

- Florists

- Clothing

- Car repair

- Hotel stays

- Dry cleaning

The book discounts will depend on the area that the book covers. One Entertainment Book may offer supermarket discounts. Another may offer dry cleaning discounts. To view and/or purchase the book in various areas, access www.entertainment.com or visit a local bookstore.

Some establishments or schools may also sell them as fund-raisers. They usually have several discounts, including groceries, retail, attractions, and restaurants. Their content typically provides an adequate variety. As mentioned with other coupon books, you should review the coupons because some restrictions may apply.

Some areas have advertisement books with coupons. You can find them in retail and grocery stores. Some arrive via the mail. These booklets contain a variety of discounts, including coupons for bagels, pizzas, restaurants, and so forth.

Coupons in the Mailbox

Your mailbox is another place to find grocery and local vendor coupons. Manufacturers will sometimes mail coupons for their product with an enclosed sample. To get on mailing lists to receive coupons and incentives via mail, call the company. The phone number is usually on the product's packaging. The packaging may include an e-mail address. Some companies allow you to enroll online for promotions.

Stores will print coupons on store circulars enclosed in the newspapers. Grocery and other local merchant circulars distributed by the United States Postal Service (USPS) may contain coupons. Some papers may send a monthly booklet with retail store coupons enclosed. Some grocery stores deliver smaller circulars to residences. These may include triple coupons or discounts on fresh meats, breads, or fresh vegetables.

Coupons in Magazines

Manufacturer coupons can also be found inside many magazines. Some magazines, for example, *Woman's Day* and *Family Circle*, may periodically include a booklet of coupons in the centerfold. Other magazines may include coupons on various pages throughout the magazine.

Coupons in Physician's Offices

Your doctor's office may have coupons specific to his or her specialized area of medicine. These are available to patients throughout the waiting room. For example, a pediatrician may have coupons for a children's cold remedy product. A podiatrist may have coupons for foot cream.

Coupons in Miscellaneous Places

You can find other places to find coupons for products besides grocery items. Restaurant placemats may offer coupons for several services and activities. Some may be printed on the bags of a child's meal at a fast-food restaurant. Inside the green section of some telephone books are various coupons for food, services, homes, and so forth. The children's section of some libraries, elementary schools, and doctors' offices might have some free publications, which may include coupons for children's meals, activities, birthday parties, and so forth.

Organize, Categorize, and Compile the Coupons

To successfully organize the coupons, use a large, accordion-style organizer to help locate the coupons quicker once they are divided into categories. These organizers vary in price and can be found at craft, office supply, or department stores. Before purchasing one, verify that the sections at the bottom are sealed from one another. Sealed sections will prevent the coupons from falling through the bottom of the organizer and mixing into different categories. Many nationwide craft stores may include coupons in their advertisement circulars. These circulars are often found in the weekend paper. To begin saving money, use the discount coupon when purchasing the organizer.

You can use several methods to categorize the coupons. Our favorite is dividing the coupons into subjects, for example, meat, dairy, paper goods, frozen goods, medicines, cleaners, cereal/breads, and so forth. Another method is organizing the coupons alphabetically by product name. For example, if the product was Sure Clean detergent, it would be filed under "S." There is no set method to organize the coupons. As you collect coupons, sort them in your organizer according to your preferred method.

To compile your coupons, you will need a small coupon holder. If you intend to visit more than one store, use legal-sized envelopes for the coupons you intend to use each week after reviewing the sales circulars. When writing the grocery list, include the brand, size, and weight of the product, for example, write boneless, skinless chicken cutlets, $1.99 per pound for four–six pound packages. You can also write down all the specific information, including size and weight. In case the store does not have the sale item clearly posted, bring the circular to verify the brand and size of the item on sale. To avoid forgetting your coupons, place the envelope in your vehicle or pocketbook. After the shopping is complete, return the unused coupons to the organizer for later. By using this method, you will not need to carry the organizer into the store.

To keep the coupons up-to-date, verify expiration dates of the coupons at least bimonthly. This will help keep the coupon file from becoming overwhelming to sort through when utilizing the weekly sales. Additionally, it can be helpful to make a miscellaneous section for restaurant coupons and other non-grocery items, for example, batteries, manufacturer rebates, and so forth.

You must remember that you must go through trial and error to find the most efficient and best method that will work for you. This may mean customizing the organizer so you can locate specific coupons easily.

Chapter Two:
Getting the Most from Coupons and Rebates

Several people do not buy the weekend papers because it is just an added expense. However, by only using two or three coupons, they would have saved the equivalent of the cost of the newspaper or more. The following page provides an example of the proper combination of coupons and store sales.

The newspaper is the best source to acquire manufacturer's coupons. These six, easy steps will assure the coupons will be available and used in the most cost-effective manner.

1. To get the best prices for grocery shopping, read the circulars to compare where the best prices are located. Shopping in more than one store may often get you the best deal.

2. View the current coupon inserts enclosed with the newspaper. Match the coupons to the advertised sales in the store circular. Cut out the coupons you currently will need. Set aside the others to cut and file accordingly later.

3. Some grocery stores accept Internet coupons. In your coupons or file, if no coupons are available for a product you currently need, look on Web sites where you can print free manufacturer's coupons, which are listed in this book. Print the coupons you will currently need. Some Web sites change the coupon offers weekly.

4. Write a shopping list containing the items that will be purchased.

5. Write the name of the grocery store on the front of an envelope in case the shopping trip includes purchasing products from more than one store. Use one envelope for each store.

6.   Locate coupons in the file that coincide with the current advertised sales.

If a grocery store does not include the circular in the newspaper, check its Web site to see if one is available. If none is available, ask the customer service desk to put you put on the store's mailing list. If a store is near a relative that you visit often and it does not have a Web site, ask the service desk if you can receive a circular in your mail.

Pharmacy Coupons, Incentives, and Rebates

Some retail stores and nationwide pharmacies may print coupons in their circulars offering a gift card for transferring or filling a new prescription. If you have copays and your health insurance covers prescriptions at that location, the coupon is worth it. Read the fine print for any restrictions. On the next visit, use the coupons in conjunction with the gift card. Many pharmacies will accept competitor's coupons for the new or transferred prescription. Before you fill the prescription, ask the pharmacy if it will honor the coupon.

One nationwide pharmacy distributes cards to put on key rings to use for accumulating extra care bucks. Look in the weekly circulars to verify if the items that offer the extra care bucks are necessary for your household. Look in your file for coupons that coincide with the current offer. The extra bucks generally will be given back to you two to three days after the purchase and upon your next purchase. Look at the bottom of the receipts. Some may include coupons for money off future purchases. Other pharmacies have rebate programs and print a rebate circular. It is usually besides the weekly store in the pharmacy. If you are not sure which incentives are at the pharmacy you utilize, ask at the customer service desk.

During one week, a nationwide pharmacy advertised free gas card rebates that would be sent by mail when consumers purchased specific products shown in the circular. The pharmacy offered different levels of rebates that depended on the total purchase price. That week, rebates between $50.00 and $99.00 were entitled to a $15.00 gas card. To qualify for the rebate, a $58.11 purchase was made. Each product purchased that week was on sale. In addition, they were combined with coupons from one of the inserts that was enclosed in the newspaper that week. Refer to the following table. It will display actual purchases made that day and break down the overall savings for that particular order.

Product	Price	Coupon	Total cost
Paper towels	$0.99 each	$1.00 off two rolls	$0.50 each

Spray air freshener	Two for $5.00	$1.00 off each (Had two)	Two for $3.00
12-pack of bathroom tissue	$4.99	$1.00 off one 12-pack	$3.99
Air freshener machine	$24.95	$10.00 off	$14.95
Machine refill	$4.95	$1.00 off	$3.95
Two bottles of floor cleaner	$1.99 each	$1.00 off two	Two for $3.00
Wall erasers	$1.99 each	$1.00 off two	Two for $3.00
Cough syrup	$4.99	$1.00 off	$3.99
		Total (with tax)	$58.11
		Coupons	$18.00
		Gas card rebate	$15.00
		Total savings	$33.00
		Total cost	$25.11

The total savings does not reflect the original cost of these items because they were all on sale at the time of purchase. The coupons, which were not utilized that week, were returned to my file for later use.

Quite often, stores will advertise some sale items concurrently with items in the coupon booklets that week. Manufacturer's coupons may also be used in department stores, drugstores, and other retail stores. Manufacturer's coupons may not be accepted in conjunction with a coupon from a sale circular when the circular lists on the top of it, manufacturer's coupon as opposed to store coupon.

Not all discount stores accept coupons. Ask the cashier or customer service representative if the store accepts coupons. A local chain of grocery outlets sells food up to 70 percent off the retail price. They do accept many coupons. Located near the register is a list of a few companies that do not permit their coupons to be utilized at that chain. The store only accepts the coupons at face value because the prices are already discounted.

Some grocery stores have machines containing coupons in certain aisles. These coupons usually state that they cannot be doubled. If the item is a household item, take one anyway. The item could go on sale, and you might not have a coupon in your file. Multiple coupons might be needed for a sale, or the coupon in your file might have recently expired.

Trial Sizes

Obtain coupons that are valid on any size. Many times, the items in the trial section can be obtained at little or no cost. This is especially beneficial for vacations. Some items that have been purchased include laundry detergent, shampoo, body wash, deodorant, baby lotions, soaps, and so forth. If a child loses a trial-sized bottle of shampoo during a camping trip, it is less disappointing than losing a full-sized bottle. Trial-sized items will reduce the amount of space being used when packing.

Clearance Items

Coupons can be used on clearance items. For example, a box of single-serving flavor mixes was on clearance for 50 percent off the regular retail price, which was $2.99. The clearance price was reduced to $1.50. I had coupons in my file for $1.00 off two items. Ten boxes cost $10.00 instead of $30.00.

"Try Me Free" Offers

Many "try me free" offers are available, including at courtesy desks, on tear-off pads in aisles, or in coupon inserts in newspapers. The manufacturer's rebates usually require a bar code from the product along with the original sales receipt and rebate form. An expiration date is also on the form. Make sure they receive the receipt, bar code, and form before the printed expiration date. Many of these items will say it is free up to a certain price, depending on what was actually paid after the sale and coupon. Rebates may take up to four to six weeks.

Double and Triple Coupons

Some stores will allow consumers to double or triple manufacturer's coupons. Doubling or tripling the coupon's value will decrease the size of the bill and save more money. Establishments have different rules about doubling and tripling coupons. Some stores only allow consumers to double a certain number of coupons for the same item.

Other stores that offer to double coupons with a face value of $1.00 might limit how many coupons can be used in a single visit. Each store has a different maximum value of the coupon that it allows to be doubled. Unfortunately, some areas have stores that do not double coupons.

The triple coupons are often attached to the store circular. The maximum value allowed is printed on the coupon. When using a manufacturer's coupon with this triple coupon, look at the maximum face value that they will triple. For maximum savings, try to use double and triple coupons in conjunction with items that are currently on sale.

Purchasing Multiple Items

If a coupon is available for a nonperishable item on sale, it would be advantageous to purchase it. The expiration dates are often extensive. Verify the date on the products before you buy them. If a brand-name coffee is on sale, buy a few cans at the sale price with the discount coupons. If you do not, you may need the product later. It might not be on sale. You might also not have a coupon available. Then your grocery reserves will be useful. If you do not have a pantry or sufficient cabinet space, install shelving where space is available. You can also purchase a storage unit with doors to maintain your overstock of groceries. The best way to purchase a product is if it can be combined with a sale and a coupon. A leading misconception about using coupons is the notion that you should buy something because you have a coupon for it for that week. If the item is not on sale and you are solely purchasing it because a coupon is available, then there is a good chance that it is not worth buying.

For example, a brand-name cereal costs $2.49 for one box. You have a coupon for $1.00 off two boxes. With the coupon, you will spend $3.98 for buying two boxes. The following week, the same cereal might be advertised for $2.00 a box. Now two boxes will cost $3.00. By using the coupon that was put aside from the prior week, you saved $0.98.

Some stores advertise that, if you buy four boxes of a brand-name cereal, you will automatically receive $6.00 off the cereal order. These purchases can be combined with manufacturer's coupons. The brand-name cereal combined with the coupons usually equates to a little over $1.00 for each box. Cereal often has a reasonable shelf life, but it is still a good idea to verify the date on the box.

Combining Coupons

Some stores allow combining store and manufacturer's coupons. If the store has Catalina coupons, the coupon tapes that are sometimes printed and given with the receipt at the grocery stores, those are not supposed to be used in conjunction with a manufacturer's coupon of an identical item. If the top of the coupon does not indicate manufacturer's coupon, that is, it states store coupon, then it can be combined with a manufacturer's coupon. Only one manufacturer's coupon can be used per item.

Rain Checks

If a product was not in stock at the store, ask the customer service area for a rain check. Look at the rain check to verify how long it is valid in that particular store. Many stores have different policies regarding expiration dates, which can range on average from one week to three months. The rain check can be used in conjunction with the coupon. If a coupon was in the grocery circular and a rain check was issued, some stores will honor the store coupon with the sale. For example, a supermarket had a sale on a brand-name soda. It advertised four twelve-packs for $10.00. In the weekly grocery circular, a vendor coupon stated I could get three two-liter bottles free when the four twelve-packs were purchased of that same soda. Because my desired flavor was sold out, I got the rain check for the four twelve-packs for $10.00. I used the coupon for the three free two-liter bottles, which originally was only valid for the week the soda was on sale. At the beginning of the shopping order, make sure the cashier knows a rain check is being used. This will prevent the product from being scanned at the regular price. When obtaining a rain check, if there was a coupon for that item, keep the rain check and the coupon together for a future purchase.

Manufacturer and Vendor Rebates

While shopping, ask if the store offers rebate programs. Usually, you have to visit a Web site to submit them online or mail in the rebates. It is much better to register rebates on the Internet because the receipt does not need to be relinquished. By using the Internet, the time to receive the rebate check is much quicker. Many people say they mail in rebates, but they never get the refund. In order to get the refund, everything that is required on the rebate form must be included. If anything is missing, the company might mail a letter requesting the missing items, but some companies will simply not send the check. Read the fine print on every rebate. If a company offers toll-free numbers or Web sites to track the product, these should be used if the rebate has not been received within an appropriate amount of time. Make a copy of your receipt, the bar code, and the rebate sheet. If a company has not received the submissions, it may request that you send a copy to them. The following sample displays information and requests that are usually included on many rebates.

Sample Mail-In Rebate

Name_____

Address_____

Phone number_____

Attach the UPC below (proof of purchase)
Include an original receipt dated between ____&_____ with the dates
circled. Offer expires on ____.

Send to:
Company name
Street address
Town, city, and zip code

In-store rebates are offered in many stores, including grocery stores, office supply stores, pharmacies, hardware stores, and so forth. If there is a rebate from a store as well as a vendor, if a duplicated receipt is not printed, ask the cashier to print a duplicate or make a copy to send in for the store rebates.

For example, while purchasing a computer, the store was offering a rebate on the computer through a major electronics chain. In addition, the computer manufacturer was offering mail-in rebates on the computer items. When doing this type of rebate, verify which rebate accepts the original bar code and original receipt. One of the two rebates might list "original bar code only." Some stores may copy the receipts for both the vendor and manufacturer's rebates. Other stores may only print one copy. The consumer must make a personal copy for the vendor rebate. On our computer purchase, six rebates were valued at $500.00. We received all the refunds and sent them to the stores and vendors. When sending in rebates, make copies just in case the company stated it never received them.

Coupon Trains

The practice of trading coupons is very beneficial. Many people do not realize that manufacturers print different denominations on the coupons based on the location where the manufacturers distribute the coupons. For example, some stores in Virginia have different rules than Pennsylvania. Because the supermarkets do not triple coupons as often in Virginia, the denomination will be different. The coupon in the Pennsylvania paper will say $1.00 off a purchase of two items. The same coupon in a newspaper in Virginia would be $0.50 off one item.

When stores in Pennsylvania do offer triple coupons, the $0.50 coupon will be worth $1.50 off one.

Many coupon trains are on the Internet.

Yahoo!		Google	
1.	Visit the Yahoo! home page.	1.	Visit the Google home page.
2.	Click **Groups**.	2.	Type "**coupon trading**" in the search box.
3.	Type "**coupon train**" in the search box.	3.	Click **Search**.
4.	Click **Search**.		

Some printable coupon sites may also list groups where individuals seek to trade coupons.

If anyone decides to join, verify the train is trading the coupons as opposed to selling them. Once you join, you can make a wish list of desired coupons and trade unwanted coupons for ones you will use for free. Beware of online coupon scams for purchasing coupons.

Coupon Trades

If friends or family utilize coupons, it may be beneficial to trade with them. Not everyone utilizes the same coupons. What might be useless to one person may be another person's treasure. Trading with friends and family will also benefit when multiple coupons are needed. I needed extra coupons for breakfast items, and my friend needed extra pet coupons. After a trade, I obtained an extra coupon from a family member who did not use the product. The three coupons resulted in a significant savings as seen in the actual purchase made below.

Three brand-name boxes of breakfast items were on sale for $4.98. I obtained three coupons worth $0.50 apiece. The store offered triple coupons that week, so each coupon was tripled to $1.50. The three coupons combined deducted a total of $4.50. Each item was $0.16, so the total bill was $0.48.

In Long Island, New York, one store doubles $1.00 coupons. If someone goes to that particular store and uses a $1.00 coupon, then the coupon value actually is $2.00 off one item. If the person uses it with an item that is on sale, he or she can usually get the items at a significant savings. For example, one purchase made from this store was for Crock-Pot liners. The liners were on sale for $1.99. The $1.00 coupon was doubled to $1.99. The register would not double it to $2.00

because that would result in a negative balance. Therefore, the product was free. The coupon obtained from Pennsylvania newspaper was $1.00 off a purchase of one item. Other areas for the same product that week were printing coupons for $1.00 off a purchase of two items. This is why trading with someone in a different state may actually be beneficial. There is no rule that coupons are exclusive to the state in which they are distributed.

Chapter Three:
Recognizing Good Sales and Shopping for Less

This chapter will educate consumers about price gimmicks that can often give the illusion of items being a good price.

Manipulative Advertising

Stores will often advertise "buy one, get one free" offers. These ads are sometimes legitimate, but stores can deceive customers with these offers. This is one instance where it is beneficial to know prices. Many stores will double the price of the item and then advertise it as "buy one, get one free." For example, boneless, skinless chicken breast is frequently sold at $1.99 per pound. The sale is advertised as "buy one, get one free." On the package, the price per pound is labeled as $3.99. The merchant doubled the price to get the consumer to buy two at regular price.

To familiarize yourself with prices, write down a few prices of the items most commonly purchased for your household. Keep this record with your list of coupons. Because meats are usually the most costly items on the food bill, start with these. Pay attention to the cost of specific items, for example, chicken breast, pork loin, and ground beef, when they are not on sale. This will help you determine if the product is really being sold at a sale price or if the unit price was really doubled. Each week, record the advertised price per pound for your selected items. When looking at meat packages, view the cost of the meat per pound, that is, the unit price. This will help you distinguish if it was doubled or if it is truly a "buy one, get one free" offer.

Store club unit price	You buy	You pay
$5.99 per pound	2.77 pounds	$16.59

Some people may not understand how to read the label. Above is a label of a recently purchased meat. The numbers shown on the lower-left corner, above the sell by date, is the net weight. The net weight is the total weight of the meat. The unit price is the price per pound, that is, the price the customer is being charged. The amount on the right-hand side is the total cost of the package. If the item is on sale with a bonus card, there may be a tag below it that indicates the adjusted cost of the item.

A store will sometimes offer coupons on the fresh meat of your choice. For example, a store printed a coupon on the back of its circular for $3.00 off a $15.00 meat purchase. Combining sale, club card, and coupon, the total savings on this New York strip steak was $13.25. After discounts, the final cost was $13.59 for nearly three pounds of steak.

Over time, the sale prices will become more familiar, and you will know if it is a good sale or not. Also, when buying items such as ground beef, realize cheaper is not always better. The percentage listed on the label refers to fat content. When you purchase meat that is labeled 70–75 percent, you are paying for a higher quantity of fat (25–30 percent), which will cook away when you use it. This would be like buying four quarter-pound burgers and throwing one away. That might not seem like all that much until you think of it on a larger scale. If this were one hundred pounds of meat, twenty-five pounds would be waste. Even though it is less expensive at the outset, this is obviously not a very good buy. Butchers may sometimes distribute coupons to purchase high-quality meat at a significant savings. If none are in the area, try to purchase nothing lower than a minimum of 85 percent. Higher percentages on the packages result in a lower fat content, hence less waste.

Store-brand Products versus Name-brand Products

Though not always the case, consumers can generally save money by purchasing store-brand items. Major meat and poultry companies will usually package their products under the store name and then sell them at a discount. The store-branded chicken is approximately $0.20 a pound cheaper than the same product packaged under the brand name. In this case, the consumer is only paying more because of the label on the wrapper, not because of the superior quality of the product in the wrapper.

If the Sunday paper includes coupons for brand-name meats, try to use them in conjunction with a sale to significantly reduce meat expenses. Recently, a grocery store had a sale on a brand-name sausage. The packages were on sale for two for $3.99. By trading with family and friends, I had obtained multiple coupons, each with a face value of $1.00 off each eighteen-ounce package. I was able to purchase six packages for slightly more than $6.00. The packages that were not consumed that week were frozen for a week when sausage prices might be too high.

When it comes to nonperishable items, the store-brand products are not necessarily the better choice. The store-brand cookies might be $1.29 while the brand-name cookies may be $1.79. If there is a $0.50 coupon and the store doubles the manufacturer's coupons, then the price of the brand-name cookie will only be $0.79. Therefore, the brand-name item actually becomes less expensive than the store-brand product. If the store happens to be tripling coupons that week, your cost can be as low as $0.29 per bag. If you have extra coupons for the cookies in the file, try to use them when the store is advertising triple coupons that week and has an item on sale. Not only will the cookies be purchased at a great price with sale and coupons, they can also be saved for future household use or a child's birthday party at school. You can also donate them to a school, church, or a local food pantry. Someone with an abundance of cookie bags might choose to donate to a food drive or surprise a friend by bringing them a tray of cookies. I have seen brand-name cookies go on sale for $1.50 a bag. That brand-name cookie pouch had a $0.50 coupon, thus making it free.

Fresh Produce

Another way to save on fresh produce is by going to flea markets or fruit stands in the area. Recently, a local grocery store was charging $0.59 cents a pound for bananas. The flea market had them at four pounds for $1.00. Purchasing the vegetables on sale and freezing them for later use can be beneficial, especially if they will no longer be in season soon. Meals have often been planned according to the food that was on sale that week. Some weeks have very good sales while other weeks can be very disappointing. During weeks when the sales are not to my liking, I will utilize the food that I previously froze. If you have a basement or garage, an extra freezer would be a good investment.

Comparison Shopping

Sunday papers offer a vast number of circulars to assist in comparison shopping from the comfort of your home. National warehouses, which require memberships, do not offer circulars in newspapers. If you are a member, compare prices. The time and effort will be well spent if the result is a significant savings. Some national warehouses will occasionally mail a one-day pass to nonmembers. Rather than discarding it, use it as an opportunity to compare prices. Look at products that are normally bought for the home because those prices are probably most familiar.

If you are comparing food items, check the prices in the grocery circulars. Consider the coupon savings and rebates, where applicable. In addition, equate the ounces to equal amounts and subtract the applicable number of coupons. If you are unsure how to figure out which product is the better buy, a later chapter lists a Web site that includes a calculator specifically designed to do these figures.

Warehouse versus Small Retail Stores

Electronics, DVDs, CDs, books, and other items are usually reasonably priced at warehouses. To ensure you are obtaining it at the best price, compare it with retail stores that sell the identical items to verify which merchant has the better price after sale and rebates.

The electronics section had better prices in the warehouse than offered in the office supply store. That week, an all-in-one machine for a computer was on sale at the warehouse for $44.88. The same name and model number in a national office supply store was priced at $79.95. No rebates were offered at either store for the product. The receipt was brought back to the national office supply store. The office supply store did offer to match the price of the warehouse if it was the exact product. Because there was no circular showing the price, the office supply store offered to call the store to verify the price. When the office supply store called and confirmed that it was the same product, make, and model number, the receipt was adjusted to match the warehouse price. A refund of $30.00 was issued. When comparing prices, it is also beneficial to view prices at companies online.

Many chain warehouses do not take manufacturer's coupons. If you are shopping at a warehouse and are unsure if manufacturer's coupons are accepted, ask at the courtesy desk. I am aware of only one chain that accepts them. Occasionally, some warehouses may offer booklets of coupons that are exclusive in their establishment.

It is occasionally true that buying bigger quantities can save you money. It depends greatly on the items being purchased. For some food items, a larger quantity does not always mean a better value. If items are on sale and a coupon is available for the item, it might be worth calculating to see where the better value can be obtained. The following are actual examples taken from a warehouse located in Pennsylvania on October 31, 2005, and a nearby grocery store. This comparison was done with the same brand-name cereal. The only difference was the size. The box at the warehouse held 37.0 ounces. Three boxes at the grocery store equaled 38.7 ounces.

Nationally Known Warehouse	Large Chain Grocery Store
The final cost was $5.27 for 37.0 ounces.	The cereal was on sale at 12.9 ounces for $2.00. Three boxes cost $6.00. That week, coupons at the courtesy desk offered discounts of $1.10 for each box. I used three coupons. Subtracting $3.30 from $6.00, my total cost was $2.70 for 38.7 ounces.

This was a significant savings by utilizing the sale in conjunction to the coupons. Also, buying it at the grocery store in three separate boxes, as opposed to one big box, reduces the chance of the cereal getting stale once it was opened. The warehouse did not accept manufacturer's coupons.

The key to getting the best prices is to recognize prices of items and comparison shop to know when a product is worth buying.

Chapter Four:
More Ways to Save Money and Obtain Free Items

Another great source for acquiring coupons is the Internet. This chapter lists many useful Web sites where coupons can be printed. Sites often change the coupon offers, so check back regularly. Before using coupons printed from the Internet, check with local merchants to see if they accept them. Some merchants no longer accept Internet coupons because some dishonest people tampered with them by changing the amounts and/or product names.

In addition to coupons, many companies offer numerous incentives, including free checks for baby formula, free formula by mail, free magazine subscriptions, free samples of pet food, and so forth. This chapter will list several Web sites and/or phone numbers to contact to sign up for promotions.

New Residents

If relocating to a new town, visit the Welcome Wagon at www.welcomewagon.com for coupons valid at local merchants in the area. If no one in the household has ever applied to the Welcome Wagon and you own a home, apply for it. The coupons offered depend on the area. In my town, I was entitled to the following free services: a haircut, car inspection, emissions testing, thermometer from the hospital, and coupons at a local grocery store. These welcome packages often contain many valuable in-store coupons. Remember to pay attention to the expiration dates or any other restrictions that may apply. Quite often, a welcome package can take up to four to six weeks after registering before it is received.

Discount Club Cards

When moving into a new residence, sign up for discount club cards. They can be acquired from a multitude of merchants, including supermarkets, CVS pharmacies, Ace Hardware, vitamin stores, Hallmark, bookstores, office supply stores, and some nurseries. The office supply store cards are also very helpful for earning back money for business owners.

Freebies

The following is a partial list of Web sites where consumers can obtain money-saving offers. These sites will offer a vast number of coupons, rebates, discounts, and much more on a wide array of items. These sites are not only limited to grocery items. (Web sites commonly change their offers, so periodically check for new ones.)

Web site	Description
www.coolsavings.com	• Print free coupons, merchant savings, and much more
www.slickdeals.net	• Provides a large list of coupons, price searches for a vast variety of products, including video games, electronics, movies flowers, gourmet, apparel, technology and much more
www.freeafterrebate	• Lists items that could be received free after rebate
www.couponcraze.com	• Provides a multitude of coupons, including music, sports, recreation, office supply, toys, games, jewelry, home, garden, and much more
www.couponcabin.com	• Offers printable coupons and codes for coupons to apparel, retail, gift, and other merchants These discounts include many upscale stores.
www.savings-center.com	• Offers many freebie items and store coupons
www.couponmountain.com	• Offers coupons from numerous merchants, including Dell, HP, Target, Staples, Office Depot, Linens 'n Things, and much more
www.dealpluscoupon.com-retrieve	• Offers coupons and discount codes
www.dailyedeals.com	• Offers great deals on many items including "as seen on TV" products, sports, bedding, home electronics, perfumes, household, and advertised daily deals

www.all-freemagazines.com	• Provides list of free magazine subscriptions available
www.boodle.com	• Offers free printable coupons
www.refundsweepers.com	• Offers more than six hundred free products and samples • Offers coupons and deals for over two hundred stores
www.omeda.com	• Offers a free three-year subscription to Remedy magazine to people over forty years old
www.techbargains.com	• Offers discounts on a wide range of electronics, including cheap digital cameras, discounted computers, laptops, MP3 players, and more
www.ilovefreebies.com	• Offers free samples, coupons, and more
www.absolutelyfreebies.com	• Provides a list of available freebies, including catalogs, clip art, Web pages, freeware, screensavers, and much more
www.collegefreestuff.com	
www.freemania.net	• Offers printable coupons for the following categories: grocery, retail, baby, entertainment, theme parks, clothing, health, medicine, beauty, and cosmetics • Provides list of where to acquire free samples
www.welovefreebies.com	• Offers a large variety of freebies, including clothing, accessories, baby items, posters, recipes, cookbooks, cards, health and beauty, fonts, phones, ring tones, and much more
www.coupons.com	• Offers free printable grocery coupons
www.fatwallet.com	• Offers free online coupons, promotional offers, and discount prices at hundreds of merchants
www.quicktoclick.com	• Offers many computer codes for discount coupons, including airlines, car rentals, and several retail merchants
www.savingsadvice.com	• Offers grocery coupons, grocery price converter, recipes, financial advice, money-saving tips, investing and banking answers, freebies, and much more

www.sallybeauty.com-online	• Offers beauty supply product coupons Licensed cosmetologists can obtain additional savings.
www.eversave.com	• Offers free grocery coupons, recipes, and free samples
www.hotcoupons.com	• Provides coupons from local, regional, and national businesses
www.mycoupons.com	• Provides free printable coupons, coupon codes, special promotions, popular offers, and so forth
www.freebiesplanet.com	• Offers free coupons, catalogs, CDs, clip art, e-mail, jokes, food, music, beauty, health, and more
www.planetfreebie.com	• Offers free coupons, rebates, PC freebies, music freebies, books, magazines, scripts, software products, and more
www.shopping-bargains.com	• Provides online coupons, codes, and bargains for more than one thousand online stores.
www.bargains4-you.com	• Offers grocery and a wide array of retailer coupons, coupon clippers, coupon surfer, and club mom • Provides sites of interest for teachers and health and fitness professionals
www.valuepage.com	• Offers more than one thousand free things, coupons, grocery coupons, and more
www.ultimatecoupons.com	• Offers coupon codes and coupons for a comprehensive list of merchants
www.couponbug.com	• Offers free printable manufacturer's coupons for popular grocery items
www.howamazing.com	• Offers free music, games, graphics, and more
www.freecycle.org	• Provides a way to find freebies in your local area
www.lowprice4U.com	• Offers more than one hundred freebies to choose from
www.thefreesite	• Offers a large variety of free items, including free stuff for cell phones, free sounds, graphics, games, fonts, business freebies, chat services, and much more

| www.couponseven.com | • Offers coupons from a broad spectrum of popular merchants |
| www.flamingoworld.com | • Offers printable and online coupons, rebates, clearance items, comparison pricing, weekly ads, and much more |

More Grocery Coupons and Free Recipes, Coupons, and Newsletters

Many grocery sites offer coupons, recipes, newsletters, magazines, and so forth. The following is a small list of popular companies that offer a variety of incentives. If there is a product that you use in your household and it is not listed, check the packaging for a Web site or a phone number to request coupons.

Web site	Description
www.turkeyhill.com	• Call (800) MY-DAIRY for a free calendar with Turkey Hill drink and ice cream coupons
www.kraft.com	• Sign up for a free magazine subscription and occasional coupons
www.stonyfield.com	• Offers free coupons, newsletters, and recipes
www.splenda.com	• Offers free recipes
www.icecreamusa.com	• Offers free recipes
www.verybestbaking.com	• Offers free recipes
www.bettycrocker.com	• Offers free recipes and e-newsletter
www.landolakes.com	• Offers free recipes and promotions
www.campbellkitchen.com	• Offers free recipes
www.cairo.com	• Check local sales circular

Giving Gifts

With all the products bought at sale prices, people can take advantage of their overstock by making up gift baskets for different occasions. If someone is having a baby, a basket filled with baby items can be assembled. Several places are available to buy baskets at a reasonable price. Some craft circulars offer 40–50 percent off one regularly priced item in the store. Garage sales are also good places to check. If you do not want to use a basket, a gift bag is another option. These can be found at many dollar stores or discount stores. When using the coupons, it is easy to fill up a basket of baby lotion, wipes, powder, and many other infant necessities. To complete the package, a dollar store often carries cellophane. This wrap provides coverage and will look attractive while being practical.

Recently, a baby basket was assembled using coupons and purchasing all the contents on sale. Six brand-name baby coupons were obtained that were worth $1.50 each. A gift bag was purchased. Inside the bag were baby wash, baby lotion, baby wipes, baby liquid powder, and soap-filled washcloths. Purchasing the items on sale and using the coupons brought the purchase to a total of $6.00. If none of the items were on sale and no coupons were available, these items were calculated to cost approximately $25.00.

If you do not have any friends or family with a baby, a parish that collects baby items for mothers-in-need would gladly accept the donation. Another basket idea may be for someone with a severe cold or the flu. He or she would appreciate a basket filled with a couple of cans of chicken soup, tissues, and possibly cough drops or vapor rub.

Several coupons are offered for makeup. It can be used for a teenage girl who may be having a birthday party. Drugstores often have good sales on makeup. Combining coupons with the sale items, a basket can be filled with lipstick, blush, eyeliner, mascara, and so forth. it would be highly appreciated and accomplished at a minimal cost.

Recently, there were coupons for board games in the manufacturer's coupons. Each coupon was valued between $2.00 and $3.00. A nationwide toy store had the games advertised as "buy one, get one free." Purchase the items during the sale and in conjunction with the coupons. This will allow games to be on hand for when a child comes home from school with an unexpected invitation to a party or for giving gifts during a holiday season. If there are no children in the household or relatives with small children, they can be purchased and donated to a charitable organization.

The holidays are usually very stressful for many people. They have to budget gift purchases in conjunction with their bills. It may be beneficial to plan to store gifts in advance for birthdays or the holidays. Spring and summer are ideal times to utilize the 40–50 percent off coupon in the craft circulars. Many kits are available to purchase, including woodworking, building model cars, or making jewelry, candles, and soap. Storing gifts in a closet each month can result in making the holidays a lot more enjoyable. It makes it easier if people do not have to fret over the bills while searching for extra money to buy gifts.

After the holidays, it is a good idea to stock up on all the necessities for the following year. When the holiday season is over, wrapping paper, gift tags, and other holiday items usually get discounted 75–90 percent off the retail price. Buying the items in advance will help defray the costs of purchasing those items at regular retail price the following year. If storing the items is a problem, there are storage holders for wrapping paper, tape, ribbon, and bows.

Baby Products

Baby companies often send checks for baby formula and coupons for free formula via the mail as an incentive for purchasing their items. You can call or send an e-mail to the following companies to start saving on baby products. If the company used for baby items in the household is not listed, look on the label or packaging of the formula, baby food, diapers, or accessory for more information.

Web site	Description
www.pampers.com	• Register codes from diaper packages for free merchandise • Offers money-saving coupons
www.babycenter.com	• Offers a quarterly magazine, coupons, special offers, and e-newsletters
www.beechnut.com	• Call (800) 233-2468 to receive a free e-newsletter, feeding tips, nutrition tips and more
www.huggies.com	• Call (888) 525-8388 for coupons
www.enfamil.com	• Call (800) 222-9123 to receive checks, information booklets, and, occasionally, free formula via mail
www.gerber.com	• Call (800) 443-7237 for free coupons
www.verybestbaby.com	• Call (800) 284-9488 for coupons
www.americanbaby.com	• Offers a free magazine subscription for new parents.
www.brightbeginnings.com	• Offers free baby formula sample, parenting tips, coupons, giveaways, and contests
www.earthsbest.com	• Offers free feeding guide, coupons, promotions, and offers
http://babyresource.com	• Offers printable coupons, coupon codes, restaurant coupons, and more
www.babystep.com	• Offers free software and downloads for expecting parents

www.babiesonline.com	• Offers many free baby incentives, including a free baby journal, baby announcements, free six-month subscriptions to two magazines, and more

Phone Number	Description
(800) 526-3967	• Call Johnson & Johnson to receive a new parent pack
(877) UL-4-SAFE	• Call to receive free home safety tips
(888) 935-5543	• Call for free Triaminic information
(800) 638-2772	• Call to receive a free safety checklist for taking care of children
(888) 344-BABY	• Call to receive a free color booklet about child's development from birth to eighteen months
(800) 833-4121	• Call to receive money-savings checks on Good Start Supreme formula

Restaurants

Some restaurants allow coupons to be used in conjunction with their reward card to accumulate points. The amount of points earned will determine the discount for which the reward card holder is eligible. For example, you could receive a free appetizer or meal. By signing up for a reward card, discounts may also come via mail for money off an entrée. This may occur if the company has noticed the reward card has not been active for a certain length of time. Some restaurants that include these incentives are Charlie Brown's, Crab Barn, and TGI Friday's.

Birthday Incentives

Many restaurants have birthday clubs people can join. Most will have no charge to enroll. After signing up, a gift certificate or coupons will be sent to each member of the family that appears on the application. This can be used around the time of the person's birthday to pay fully or partially for the meal and/or a dessert. While some restaurants may restrict the birthday club to children only, others will offer it to every member of the family. The application will show if there any age stipulations. Some restaurants may send incentives on a couple's anniversary. Some of the establishments with these clubs are:

All American Cafe
Applebee's

Arner's
Austin Grill
Bennigan's
Bob Evan's
Burger King
Cactus Willies
Charlie Brown's
Crab Barn
Fuddrucker's
Hooter's
Hoss's Steak House
IHOP
Krispy Kreme
Marie Calenders
Old Country Buffet
Olive Garden
Outback Steakhouse
Perkin's
Red Lobster
Red Robin
Shoney's
TGI Friday's
The Vine Tavern
Tony Roma's
Wendy's

Many establishments offer birthday clubs, so check with a local restaurant to see if one is offered. For example, even though they are a chain, McDonald's, Burger King, and Wendy's are three examples of a restaurant that might not have a birthday club. It all depends on the person owning the franchise. If the company offers a birthday club, it will be advertised within the establishment.

When you join the birthday club at Hollywood Video, you will receive a free movie rental on your birthday. If needed, sign up for a free membership card from them. Some stores will verify the information from the card to distribute the free rental. Other locations may ask to see your driver's license. The other free movie rentals are at the following locations: Safeway Grocery Stores, Food Pavilion Grocery Store, and Harkins.

Other birthday incentives include the following:

- Some national chain ice cream stores offer incentives for birthdays. For example, members of Cold Stone Creamery's birthday club receive free ice cream on their birthday. You can visit a store or www.coldstonecreamery.com to sign up. At Baskin-Robbins, you can have two-and-a-half ounces of ice cream and $3.00 off a birthday cake. Sign up for the birthday club at www.baskinrobbins.com.

- If a new baby is in the household, visit the bakeries at the local supermarkets. Many will offer a free birthday cake for a child on his or her first birthday. Ask the local supermarket bakery if a free birthday cake for a child's first birthday is offered.

- You can get a free car wash at Scrub-a-Dub on your birthday. For locations, visit www.scrubadub.com.

- At http://familyinternet.about.org, you can print birthday invitations and envelopes at no charge.

- For free skiing or riding at Bear Mountain or Snow Summit on your birthday, visit www.bearmountain.com or call (909) 866-5766. You must show identification to prove your birthday.

- Some nurseries offer birthday clubs. For example, at a garden center located in two counties in the southeastern part of Pennsylvania. You receive a free plant during the month of your birthday and a $5.00 certificate for every $100.00 spent when you sign up for its reward club. Check with the local nursery to verify if incentives are offered.

E-Cards

For someone who deserves a friendly greeting, encouragement, or birthday salutation, just send a free e-card. Many free programs are on the Internet, including www.riversongs.com, www.hallmark.com, and www.greeting123.com.

If you do not want to use e-cards, you can buy a card-making program, make your own personalized cards, and mail them. The programs are inexpensive and easy to use. They also give a more personalized touch than store-brand cards. Many of these programs will include the ability to make personalized labels, calendars, photo cubes, scrapbooks, and more. When making cards, buy a heavier stock paper. It will give the card a better texture, and the ink will not bleed through. The card will look and feel the same as a higher-quality card. When buying paper, try to buy extra when it is on sale. During the major holiday seasons, paper will often be put on sale. If available, use the coupon with the sale.

Recipes

For anyone looking for special recipes for people with dietary restrictions or just something different to cook, many free recipes are available. If someone has a health problem, go to the Web site that deals with the specific medical condition. For example, visit www.diabetes.org, http://heartburn.about.com, www.cholesterol.about.com, or www.americanheart.org.

Check products under their brand name. For example, look for Splenda under www.splenda.com to find several recipes to help lower sugar intake. Other Web sites with free recipes include www.foodtv.com, www.teleport.com, www.recipegoldmine.com, www.ichef.com, www.fatfree.com, www.mealtime.org, www.betterhomesandgarden.com, www.cureyourheartburn.com, www.olivegarden.com, www.pam4you.com, www.recipes.com, www.kraft.com, and www.jiffymix.com. At the Kraft Web site, you can receive a free magazine subscription with recipes and occasional coupons. These are just a couple of sites. Many others are available. If there is a product used regularly in the household, check if a Web site is listed on the package. The Web sites generally will display coupons, recipes, points, or incentives offered.

For free cookbooks, you can visit www.healthrecipes.com, www.nancyskitchen.com, or www.freeandclearstuff.com.

Medical Advice and Help

If you want free medical advice or information on a specific condition, visit some of following Web sites:

Web site	Description
www.dermadoctor.com	• Offers advice on skin problems
www.ultimate-cosmetics.com	• Offers beauty advice for hair, skin, and so forth
www.keepingkidshealthy.com	• Provides pediatric and parenting advice
www.merckadvice.com	• Provides medical information and advice on many conditions
www.mayoclinic.com	• Provides free medical information and more
www.healthbanks.com	

If you do not have health insurance or the cost of mammograms is not covered under your health plan, call (800) 4-CANCER or the American Cancer Society at (800) ACS-2345.

Educational Material

The following Web sites provide free educational material:

Web site	Description
www.schoolexpress.com	• Offers free activities, awards, games, and worksheets
www.abcteach.com	• Offers free worksheets, theme units, word puzzles, and so forth
www.sitesforteachers.com	• Offers free high-quality teaching resources

Incentives on Books, CDs, and DVDs

At Barnes & Noble bookstores, you can sign up for a membership card and receive a certificate worth 10 percent off all purchases. It may also be used for purchases at the café. There is a membership fee.

By visiting www.amazon.com, you can buy a variety of merchandise, including books, electronics, CDs, and DVDs. Signing up for their credit card entitles you to receive $30.00 toward your first purchase.

Visit www.half.com for good deals on books, music, and movies. You can also sell unwanted merchandise.

Borders offers a free membership card. Anyone signing up for the membership is entitled to promotions for club members, coupons printed on receipts and/or sent via e-mail. Also, when $150.00 is spent a Borders Buck certificate, worth $5.00 will be mailed. This must be used within 45 days. The other rewards available are in-store discounts printed on the register receipt and discount coupons sent to e-mail, if one was given, on the account.

For free e-books, visit www.baen.com. Science-fiction and fantasy books are included in their selection.

To receive a free Bible study guide on CD-ROM, visit www.bibleinfo.com. For a free Bible, visit www.lesea.com.

Tree and Plants

Many nurseries will offer coupons in local discount circulars distributed via the mail and local newspapers. Some nurseries have a mailing list. When you sign up, you may receive coupons.

When you visit www.freetreesandplants.com, workers with disabilities get jobs when you order plants. You only have to pay shipping and processing.

Chapter Five:
Vacation for Less

Reduce Travel Expenses

Traveling can be very expensive, especially if traveling with a family. There are several ways to reduce the expenses of vacationing. Some destinations can be visited at no cost. This chapter will display how utilizing coupons and incentives and visiting Web sites can be beneficial. It will also list a number of free tours available.

For discounts on airfare, hotel, and car rentals, you can use many Web sites for comparison pricing. Some popular sites include www.cheaptickets.com, www.expedia.com, www.hotels.com, www.hotwire.com, www.orbitz.com, www.priceline.com, and www.travelocity.com

These are just a few of the popular sites that offer reasonable prices. Organizations like AAA and AARP offer various travel discounts. AAA coupons will sometimes be mailed to residents for a discount on membership fees. If you are a member planning a vacation, before leaving, request a book of the area to see where attractions are located in the vicinity of your destination. Look on the Internet to see if any additional discounts for the attractions are available.

City Pass

When traveling to one of the nine major cities, visit www.citypass.com to get into a vast number of attractions for free when you purchase the card. This card is most useful if visiting an area for an extended time. The cities and areas included in these passes are Boston, New York City, Seattle, Chicago, Hollywood, Southern California, Philadelphia, and Toronto. A national warehouse sells it at a discount. It can be obtained within ten to fourteen days with standard shipping.

Go Card

Visit www.gocardusa.com if you are planning to vacation in any of the following destinations: Boston, Chicago, Los Angeles, Hawaii, Miami, Orlando, San

Diego, San Francisco, and Seattle. Once this card is purchased, it permits free admission into numerous attractions, museums, tours, and so forth. Three-, five-, and seven-day cards are available for purchase. It also includes a 20 percent discount on shopping and dining.

If vacationing is difficult due to a limited budget, visit www.fieldtrip.com. This site lists a vast number of places, including museums arboretums, zoos, tours, and more, to visit for free in the following areas: New Jersey, Eastern Pennsylvania, Connecticut, Northern Delaware, Northern Maryland, and New York.

Airline Incentives

If flying to a destination, sign up for the frequent-flyer program. The more you travel and use the card, the quicker points will accumulate to receive free airline miles. Enrolling is free.

Hotel Incentives

When booking a hotel, verify if the hotel has incentive programs to earn points. They can be redeemed for free nights, discounts, or more. The Web sites listed at the beginning of this chapter can be contacted to compare prices. For example, www.priceline.com was used to book a reservation in Los Angeles. A deluxe suite at a nationally known hotel that accommodated up to six people and offered many amenities for eight days cost around $800.00. The hotel was one mile from the airport. The trip included free transportation to and from the hotel to the airport.

Entertainment Book

The Entertainment Book is also a good source to use on vacations to save on hotels, attractions, dining, shopping, and so forth. If traveling during the summer months, wait to purchase the book until late spring. Starting in May, books will usually be marked down to half-price. The book coupons are always good until November 1.

Visit www.entertainment.com to order the book. Give ample time for shipping so it arrives before leaving for vacation. The books can be viewed online to see if any discounts would be beneficial for the vacation being planned. If you do not know if you want to purchase the book, calculate the savings to determine if they outweigh the cost of the book. The time of year will make a difference in the overall cost of the vacation. If you have any children or restrictions on when to travel, vacation during an off-peak season. The attractions will be less crowded during the off-peak season.

When going on vacation, it is a lot easier to bring driving directions from the hotels to the attractions, eating establishments, and so forth. Visit www.mapquest.com. Free to use, it makes getting around an unfamiliar area easier. If anyone is an AAA member or belongs to another automobile club, obtain driving directions from them.

We made the eating establishment decisions in advance by researching the Entertainment Book for restaurants located near each of the main attractions we visited. When we visited California, we, a family of five, saved over $300.00 by using coupons from the Entertainment Book. The coupons utilized from our Entertainment Book were as follows:

- We got one free admission at the wax museum in Hollywood after buying one general admission.

- We saved 50 percent off total bill on a bus tours in Hollywood.

- We got $5.00 off a $30.00 bill in a restaurant located in the Grauman's Chinese Theater complex.

- We got $5.00 off each admission at SeaWorld in San Diego. The coupon was good for up to six people.

- We got 50 percent off our total order in a restaurant outside Disneyland.

- We got $8.00 off admission for each admission at Universal Studios.

- We got $5.00 off a $40.00 bill in Tony Roma's restaurant in Universal Studios.

- We got one free admission after buying two admissions at the *Queen Mary* in Long Beach.

- We got $15.00 off the total bill at a Lone Star Restaurant in Long Beach.

- We got 50 percent off the total bill in a restaurant outside of Balboa Park in San Diego.

The cost for the book was only $12.50. We purchased it in May for our vacation in June. If I had purchased the book in November, the cost would have been $25.00. We used coupons from the Internet for some attractions that were not offered in the book. Our Internet coupons were $2.00 off each admission into a popular museum in Hollywood. We obtained five coupons for a total of $10.00 off.

Free Vacation Activities

While vacationing, take some free tours and print coupons to visit various attractions at no cost. Check out the following Web sites for further information:

Web site	Description
www.dpway.com	• Offers free coupons for San Francisco, Ca
www.free4allcity.com	• Offers free coupons for western Michigan
www.lasvegas-nv.com/las-vegas-coupons	• Offers free coupons for Las Vegas
www.orlandosaving.com-coupons	• Offers free coupons for Orlando
www.knoxkoupons.com	• Offers free coupons for Tennessee
www.neworleanscoupons.com	• Offers free coupons for New Orleans
www.free-attractions.com	• Lists various attractions to visit at no cost
www.tripadvisor.com	• Helps with your traveling needs
www.hersheychocolateworld.com	• Offers a free tour of Chocolate World
www.800padutch.com	• Provides areas of interest and free things to do while visiting the Pennsylvania Dutch community
www.centralparknyc.org	• Lists activities, including walking tours, music schedule, special events, educational programs, recreational programs, and so forth
www.wisconsin.gov	• Provides information on trip planning in Wisconsin, trip information, events, tours, and more
www.sfcityguides.org	• Lists and describes various walking tours
	• Provides news and events for the area as well as other pertinent information for visiting the area
www.usmint.gov	• Offers virtual tours as well as information on free tours of the US Mint

www.chicagotraveler.com	• Offers a comprehensive list of information for the Chicago area, including visitor guides, city information, accommodations, events, maps, things to do, neighborhood information, and tours
www.ohiotraveler.com	• Helps with travel plans including regional fun, festivals, attractions, and so forth
www.tourtexas.com	• Provides free brochures, list of events, fairs, and festivals, and so forth
www.districtcolumbia.com	• Lists twenty-five free things to do
www.arkansas.com	• Lists free things to do while visiting Arkansas

Some free food and wine tasting tours are available. Hershey Chocolate World is my favorite food tour. Before leaving, always order a free vacation book to set up an itinerary. It will help to better organize a schedule and help see more destinations in less time.

Seriously injured veterans can be entitled to receive a state park pass free of charge. It permits them into historic sites and recreational facilities at no cost. For further information, visit www.veterans.state.ny.us.

Chapter Six:
Incentives and Programs to Put Money Back in Your Pocket

The cost of living has made it difficult for families to make ends meet. This chapter is designed to help individuals save money by utilizing many resources and techniques. Many of these programs are free to use. Also included are how to locate and obtain coupons, applications, or certificates to reduce the cost of some expenses.

Affordable, Decent Houses

Habitat for Humanity, a worldwide-based company, helps low-income families by building affordable, decent homes that they could not afford otherwise. It helps to break the cycle of poverty and the feeling of hopelessness. Houses are sold at no profit with an interest-free mortgage. Homeowners and volunteers build the houses under trained supervision. The person applying for this program is required to put in a certain amount of hours with the organization. For further information, visit www.habitat.org, call (229) 924-6935 extension 2551 or 2552, or write:

> Habitat for Humanity
> 121 Habitat St.
> Amicus, GA 31709

Financial-Aid for Low-Income Families

There is help for buying a newer car or home, furthering education, or paying high medical expenses. There is no obligation to ever repay this money. The Community Action Program (CAP) is a federal program that is designed to help low-income families become more self sufficient without depending on help from public assistance. The CAP programs vary from state to state. Also, they many vary depending on the county and/or local government. This is a program based on government funding; therefore, the programs may be subject to change.

Some programs offered are; weatherization, utility customer assistance, domestic violence, employment services, housing, HEAT, outreach and case management, senior citizen centers and services, Head Start, emergency grants, decision making, parenting skills, multicultural scholarships, youth services, and transportation. For more information, visit www.nacaa.org or write to:

Community Action Agencies
100 17th St. NW
Suite 500
Washington, DC 20036

Community Action Program once offered a program to set up a designated savings account. They matched dollar for dollar in an account. The recipient had eighteen months to save toward the designated goal. If $2,000 was saved, CAP would match the $2,000. The money must be applied to one of the four necessities listed above. For example, if you wanted to buy a new or used car, you would pay the $2,000 from the savings account to the dealership. CAP would issue a $2,000 check to the same dealership toward the purchase. This will provide a down payment of $4,000. If you had a vehicle to offer as a trade-in, that could be applied toward the reduction of the price.

Try buying a car during a year-end clearance sale, typically around August or September. New cars must be sold to make room for the next-year models. Purchasing a car with very low miles will cost much less than purchasing a new one. These cars often come with the balance of the original warranty. An extended warranty may be offered for an additional charge. When purchasing, compare prices for the best deals.

For example, an actual purchase utilizing CAP was a two-year-old Buick Century with 21,700 miles. The original purchase price was $13,300. This included a warranty from the manufacturer for 75,000 miles or six years. The matched funds from CAP were $2,000. The funds from the savings account were $2,000. The trade-in vehicle was valued at $1,000. This reduced the price of the car by $5,000. The total cost of the car was $8,300. A local credit union issued a loan for a low interest rate. The total payment, including an extended warranty, was $209.00 per month for five years.

Own Cars or Homes Sooner

Ask if your current lender offers an accelerated program. Mortgages and/or car payments can be made biweekly instead of monthly. For example, instead of paying $1,000 a month, you could pay $500.00 biweekly. By making biweekly payments, you can make one extra payment a year. You can reduce payments by sending additional money toward the principal whenever extra funds are available.

Keep your tax refund aside for unexpected emergencies. With taxes rising, escrow payments may come up short. The extra money can offset the unexpected shortage of a mortgage due to a change in the taxes.

Home Insurance

To save money on home insurance, raise the amount of the deductible on your policy. Additional discounts may be given if deadbolts are installed or if the home has a fire extinguisher or alarm system. If the car and house are on the same policy, a multi-policy discount may be applied. Some policies may also provide a discount if a fire hydrant is within a certain distance from the home. To avoid policy increases, try not to file claims on a house. To be certain the rate on the policy is reasonable, obtain free quotes from competitive companies over the phone or on the Internet. When comparing prices, it is most beneficial to have the current policy on hand.

Veterans (Current or Honorably Discharged) Benefits

A Veterans Affairs (VA) mortgage is available to help veterans purchase a house. They provide protection from veterans from ever losing their house. A one-time enrollment fee is applicable. Ask if an agent handles VA mortgages. In some states, a discount can be given on property taxes if you are a veteran. At a VA hospital, veterans may receive free medical treatment. At VA pharmacies, prescriptions can be purchased for minimal copays. Free burial services are provided for the veteran and the spouse at designated burial grounds.

Some states offer disabled veterans many benefits, including exemption from real estate tax, free birth and death records, pensions for those paralyzed, free fishing or hunting licenses, emergency assistance, free admission to state parks, and so forth. For a detailed list of benefits, visit www.vba.va.gov or www.va.gov or call (800) 827-1000.

Transportation for Disabled American Veterans

In Pennsylvania, disabled veterans can get free transportation provided for them to and from the seven VA medical centers located throughout the state. There are also designated pickup and drop-off locations. If a veteran resides in a different state, he or she can verify if there is a similar program in that state.

Property Tax Help

Many programs can reduce a homeowner's property taxes. Each area offers different reductions. Some are available if you are a current or honorably discharged veteran. The STAR program is also available.

Disabled individuals and senior citizens can also apply for discounts on property taxes in some areas. The tax discount applications must be filed annually. Some offices may offer a Web site to download the forms. To find out if any property tax discounts are offered in your area, check with the local tax assessor's office. The number is listed in the local government section of the phone book.

Utility Help

The cost of utilities is also rapidly rising. If heating bills are a burden and you qualify by meeting the guidelines, the LIHEAP program can assist. Contact the utility company for a LIHEAP form. This is a federal program. As long as the income criteria are met, help with the heating cost will be given. Call (866) 674-6327 or visit www.liheap.org. Click the appropriate state on the map to find the local number.

To save money on electricity, keep bulbs and fixtures clean. The dirt absorbs light and reduces the efficiency. If you repaint a room or install new floors, remember that light colors will reflect more light.

Use timers or photocells that fit in outdoor fixtures to avoid forgetting to shut off the outside light. The light will automatically turn on at dusk and off at dawn.

Energy Star makes fluorescent bulbs under major manufacturer's names. A compact fluorescent bulb uses 75 percent less energy than an incandescent bulb. It can last up to thirteen times longer.

If buying new appliances, try to purchase energy-efficient appliances. They will initially cost more, but they will pay for themselves in the money saved on the electric bill. When purchasing the appliance, the energy guide label will list how much the appliance costs to run.

Many electric companies will have an online list informing the consumer which appliances use the lowest and highest amount of energy to run.

If a home needs weatherization and an elderly, low-income, or disabled person resides in the dwelling, free assistance is available from a federally funded program. The weatherization may save as much as 30 percent on heating or cooling expenses. Contact your local CAP for further information.

Two federal programs are available for low-income families to apply discounts to their phone bills as long as the income criteria are met. The income guidelines are listed at www.lifeline.gov.

Parents with Young Children

Families with children look for ways to stretch their budget to afford all the expenses of raising children. Some children wish to play instruments in school, but the cost of instruments to buy or rent is overwhelming. Some children's activities are costly to sign up for. Others need help with dental, prescription eyewear, medical, tutoring, and so forth. The following are some suggestions to ease the burden of these expenses:

Free Movies

In the summertime, some theaters show free movies to children. To find locations, visit www.amctheaters.com or www.cobbtheaters.com.

Medical Assistance

Children's Health Insurance Program (CHIP) is an insurance program designed for working families. Call (877) KIDS-NOW for information on the income guideline to see if you qualify.

The high cost of dental is a burden on many people. If you have a child that does not have dental coverage, bring him or her to an institute that offers dental courses. Certified dentists supervise the visits. Services are very reasonably priced. Some have a sheet listing their prices for services and fees.

For low-income seniors residing in Pennsylvania, call (877) PA-HEALTH to receive a complete list of free or low cost dental clinics.

Area	Phone number/Web site
Washington	(800) 992-2456 extension 6044
Oklahoma	www.health.state.ok.us/program/dental
Camden County (New Jersey)	(800) 704-9222
Champaign, Illinois	www.smilehealthy.org

Northern Virginia	www.ecnv.org
San Francisco	www.dph.sf.ca.us
	A sliding scale is only available for residents.
Los Angeles	www.aplaceofyourown.org
Chicago	www.cds.org
California	www.comda.ca.gov/dental

In Pennsylvania, more than 520 dentists have agreed to donate services to individuals who have a permanent disability, are elderly, or simply cannot afford dental care in a program called Donated Dental Care. For more information about the program, call (888) 683-9158. In western Pennsylvania, call (800) 716-8721.

Prescription glasses are very costly, but they a necessity for many individuals. Places are available to get free eye exams and high-quality free prescription glasses for low-income families. One company offering this incentive is www. sightforstudents.org. Call (800) 877-7195 for more information. Some school nurses will give the gift certificate to the parent for this program after verifying the household income. This program is available in forty-eight states. If is not offered in the local area, check with the local Lion's Club. They may be able to assist with obtaining free eyeglasses for adults and children.

Many children or elderly need immunizations but do not have any health insurance. Some locations offer free immunizations. Visit the local library. If a newsletter is available, read it to see if any organizations will offer this service to residents on a designated day. In some areas, visiting nurse centers will offer free immunizations to the elderly on scheduled days. Check with the Office of Aging or Social Service Department for a list of when and where free immunizations will be given. These are listed in the government section of the phone book.

Education Assistance

If a child is having difficulty in math or reading, there may be help. Tutoring costs are usually very expensive, but there is a way to get the help for the child. Ask the guidance counselor at the school to see what options are available. Each state has different programs.

In Pennsylvania, a program called Classroom Plus offers the child a grant of $500.00. This money never needs to be repaid. To get approved for this program, the guidance counselor needs to administer a test in the area in which the child is having difficulty. The child's score will determine if he or she qualifies. A comprehensive list of tutors participating in the program will be provided. The fees and availability will vary, depending on the tutor. Call several to see which one works best for you. After selecting a tutor, contact Classroom Plus to have the application approved before the child's services can begin. The parent is usually required to pay for the tutor in advance. When the bill reaches $500.00, the parent needs to send in the required documents and proof of payment to receive reimbursement. For an application or more information, call (800) 698-2720 or visit www.classroomplus@miu4.k12.pa.us.

In addition, many free Web sites can help children with homework.

Web site	Description
www.msn.encatra.com	• Offers a comprehensive list of homework sites for all grades and most subjects to obtain help and information • Offers free resources, including online atlas, online encyclopedia, online dictionary and much more.
www.homework-help.aol.com	• Provides homework and online tutorials
www.sciencepage.org	• Provides resources in all areas of science and science homework help
www.school.discovery.com	• Provides science fair ideas and projects
www.algebra.com	• Offers free homework help with algebra and geometry
www.freemathhelp.com	• Provides math lessons, games, lessons and much more
www.socialstudieshelp.com	• Offers help with various social studies topics • Provides assistance with writing research papers.

If a child three years of age or younger has delayed development or a confirmed disability, he or she may be eligible for the Early Intervention Program (EIP). The child will receive in-home services, vision services, nutrition services, service coordination, and more. For more information, call (518) 473-7106 or visit www.bei@health.state.ny.us. Verify with the state's health department if this program is offered.

Free Computers (Philadelphia Area)

In King of Prussia, Pennsylvania, a company will give residents a computer in exchange for a donation and two hours of voluntary service. The recipient can decide—within a reasonable amount of time—when they can donate the two hours. It will provide the following components: computer, monitor, mouse, keyboard, speakers, wiring, and modem. It will check the computer to assure it works properly. If a printer and ink are available, that will be included. Afterwards, the company just asks for the recipient to write and tell how the computer was beneficial and/or the family. Visit www.teamchildren.com, to learn more or call (610) 666-1795.

Ink Cartridge Incentives

Do not throw away the empty ink cartridges. Many office supply stores will give incentives for bringing them in to be recycled. Some office supply stores offer a free ream of paper for certain brand cartridges. Another offers a coupon worth $3.00 toward your next purchase of ink. A different chain offers a coupon on any purchase in the store. Check with the office supply store in your area to see what incentives are available.

Clothing

Clothing usually goes on clearance at the end of the season. This is when it is good to buy clothes for the following year. Children's clothing may be a little more difficult. The sizes may have to be estimated to determine which ones he or she might be wearing the following year. If estimating a child's size is too difficult, consider shopping at local clothing outlets. The outlets will sometimes offer coupon books that may be available at the customer service desk. Some of the flyers advertising the outlets may have coupons printed on them. Coupons can be found in Kid Stuff, Entertainment Books, and various fund-raiser books. Another option is to visit local consignment shops. The only clothes they accept are in near-perfect condition. Another alternative is to look at garage sales or flea markets. Many flea markets will sell new clothes for significantly less than many department stores. If a state charges tax on clothing, it may offer a tax-free week. Consider buying during that week in conjunction with a coupon for that clothing or department store. If purchasing a new pair of shoes, some stores will accept coupons in conjunction with their sales. In some areas, the Entertainment Book may offer clothing or shoe store coupons.

If a child outgrows his or her clothes or an adult no longer wishes to own an item, do not throw them away. If they are in like-new condition, bring them to a consignment shop. Adult consignment shops are not as common as children consignment shops. They also purchase videos, baby furniture, books, toys, and so forth. Most shops will pay individuals upon acceptance of the items. Others will pay a percentage of the sale of the item. While items can sometimes be carried in, other shops may require an appointment before bringing in the merchandise. Look in the phone book under consignment shops and services. If there are no consignment shops in the area, consider selling them at a garage sale. Some communities offer free setup at a local flea market on a specific day as long as you bring your own table. If that is available in your area, sell your items there. The other option is to sell them online or donate to a local charity. If donating, remember to request a receipt to utilize for a deduction on taxes.

Home Improvement and Craft Stores

If a child is interested in home improvement and/or craft projects, consider one of the following:

- Every second Saturday of the month, a national home improvement store offers a free workshop for children. It runs from 8:00 AM to 12:00 PM. No pre-registration is required.

- Every second Saturday of the month, a home improvement store offers a free workshop for children. It starts at 10:00 AM. No preregistration is required for this program.

- Every Tuesday and Thursday from 3:00 to 5:00 pm, a national craft store offers a take-and-make workshop for kids. There is no cost for this program. No preregistration is required.

- Every Saturday, a nationally known craft store offers a Kid's Club from 10:00 AM to 12:00 PM. The cost is $2.00.

- Every Monday, Wednesday, and Friday, another craft chain offers workshops for children from 10:00 to 11:00 AM. Preregistration is required. The fee depends on the project being done.

Summer Camps

Summer camps tend to be very expensive, but there are ways to cut costs. Look into what the community offers and what camps offer financial scholarships.

Some communities offer a playground camp. For example, the playground camp in my community is $30.00 for the whole summer. Children attend Monday through Friday from 9:00 AM to 12:30 PM. On Fridays, the children go to the town pool.

Read the township newsletter that is received in the mail. They sometimes have very inexpensive programs. For example, one activity offered now is only $10.00 for one day a week for six weeks of kickball. Additional children can sign up for $5.00. Many local churches may offer free day camps for a week. If there is a transportation problem, many churches will usually accommodate the family and provide free transportation.

Another option is Boy Scout camp for Boy Scouts. If the child does not have the funds to go, the Boy Scouts will help partially fund the child's camp fees. Ask the troop leader for an application. The other part of the money can be utilized from money the Boy Scout has raised as a result of their fund-raising efforts. Approximately one-third of what a Cub Scout or Boy Scout sells is applied toward his account. He can use those funds to optionally offset camping expenses.

Financial scholarships are also available at many YMCA camps. The funds distributed are based on an individual's income and outstanding medical expenses or extraordinary circumstances.

Also contact the local United Way organization to see if funding is available for sending children of low-income homes to camp.

If a child has a disability, many camps are designed for children with specific needs. Many of these camps offer scholarships to families who are in need and wish to send their children to camp. Some of the camps may be free of charge.

To find out what camps are offered locally, check in the phone books under camps-day and residential.

Parent Source is a booklet offered in many libraries and some businesses in Pennsylvania. It will list camps, various kid activities happening in the local area, coupons, and informative articles. It can also be viewed at www. parentssource.com.

Musical Instruments

Children may desire to learn to play instruments at school, but renting or buying them can be very expensive. I wanted a French horn. No one locally sold it used for less than $1,700. Renting it would be $25.00 a week, or $720.00 a year. I found a Web site selling the horn new with the case for $1,000. We bought it in 2004. Three years later, my son still uses it at school. The horn is still in great condition. It has a warranty in case of any defects. The site is www.string4less.com. Check the local newspaper under musical instruments for sale or go to www.amazon.com to see if anyone is selling an instrument. If there are free weekly publications delivered to the home, check in there, too.

If an instrument purchase is being considered, many Web sites offer free sheet music. Visit some of the sites listed:

Web site	Description
www.freesheetmusic.net	• Download free sheet music
www.music-scores.com	• Offers free sheet music
www.free-scores.com	• Offers free sheet music
www.virtualsheetmusic.com	• Offers classical sheet music
www.nissimo.com	• Offers free sheet music for all instruments
www.eliteskills.com	• Offers free music scores

Affordable College Education

Many programs are readily available to individuals with the desire to learn but limited on funds. The following are a few available programs that can be applied to offset or to get an education completely funded:

Federal Pell grant
TAP 529
NY Tuition Assistance Program (www.hesc.com)
Academic scholarships
Federal work study program
Coverdell Educational Savings Program
Educational IRAs
Lottery tuitions

By enrolling at www.UPromise.com, with your purchases of qualifying items, you will be reimbursed a portion back to your children's college education.

Stafford and Perkins loans are also available. Most financial aid programs are determined by the total income of the household. Programs are also available for veterans. Check with the financial aid office in the local university to see which programs are offered. For more information on the financial aid in your area or for applications, call (800) 4-FED-AID. To view many other financial aid programs, visit www.finaid.org.

Help for Senior Citizens and the Disabled

Seniors have many programs available to them at little or no charge. Call the local Office of Aging, which should be listed in the phone book. It can offer many services, including grocery shopping, housekeeping, bathing, home care, preparation of taxes at no charge, and so forth. Each state varies in some of the programs offered. Some programs depend on the individual's income and if he or she has family available to assist them. Some townships also offer free transportation to doctor's appointments.

If anyone is in a wheelchair, many county buses provide door-to-door service. Forms will need to be completed with the bus company. Required documentation may need to be provided.

Some colleges also offer seniors over the age of fifty-five the opportunity to audit classes free of charge or attend for a low tuition. Call colleges in the area to see if any participate in this program.

In the government pages of the phone book, look up VESID or Office of Vocation Rehabilitation. This organization helps people with disabilities to get an education and/or assistance with job placement. This program also helps veterans with job placement. This service is also based on the individual's financial needs. There is no charge for this service.

Other services include the following:

- If you know someone who is blind, free Braille bibles are available. Visit www.braillebibles.org for more information.

- If you know someone with cancer, call (800) ACS-2345 for a free *Life After Cancer Treatment* book.

- The local Office of Aging can help you locate local sites that offer free tax preparation. Call (800) 829-1040 for more information.

- A national program called Foster Grandparents provides an opportunity for seniors to work with high-risk children. Check with the local Office of Aging for the stipulations and/or guidelines. Visit www.retirementliving.com to locate the local Office of Aging address and phone number. Seniors can receive many free services.

- The California Registry, a state-licensed free referral service for seniors and their families, offers senior housing information, counseling, facility evaluations, and referrals. Call (800) 777-7575 for further information.

- Seniors who meet the guidelines for the Elderly Pharmaceutical Insurance Coverage (EPIC) program can save money on their prescriptions. For more information, call (800) 332-3742. This program is only available for New York residents over the age of sixty-five.

- The Meals on Wheels program delivers well-balanced meals to a senior's residence. The program is designed to improve the social, physical, economical, and nutritional being of the elderly. Call the local Office of Aging for further information. Call (703) 548-5558 to find the local Meals on Wheels number in the area.

- Virginia residents who are over the age of sixty and meet the income guidelines can receive a free fan. For further information, call Dominion Virginia Power at (800) 667-3000, or visit www.dom.com.

- If you know someone who is elderly or disabled and he or she needs help shoveling snow, call Snow Stoppers at (800) 366-0929. Volunteers will come to help.

- For a very small fee, these residents of Berks County, Pennsylvania, who are over the age of fifty can receive a card entitling them to free services, including tax preparation, notary, concerts, shows, health insurance, consumer counseling, use of two activity centers, discounts on various goods and services, activities, classes, and much more. For further information, call the Senior Citizen Council at (610) 374-3195.

- For those who are severely injured and/or chronically ill or in need of hope, visit www.angelsforhope.org. The organization will mail a free angel, butterfly, or smiley face to the individual.

Medical Assistance

If someone is without medical coverage because an employer does not provide it or it is too expensive, many programs are available to obtain free or reduced medicine. The following sites may be beneficial to visit:

Web site	Description
www.freemedicinefoundation.com	• If you make up to $80,000, you can still qualify for free medication.
	• Call (573) 996-3333 for a free brochure and application.
www.pparx.org	• Finds all the patient assistance programs available in your state
	• Call (888) 477-2669 for more information.
www.rxassist.org	• Call (401) 729-3284 for information or see if you qualify.
	• The address is Patient Assistant Program, 111 Brewster Street, Pawtucket, RI 02860.
www.freemedicineprogram.org	• To request an application, information, or a brochure, call (800) 921-0072 or write Free Medicine Program, PO Box 630217, Miami, FL 33163.
	• The fax number is (800) 951-4042.
www.merkhelps.com	• Call (800) 50-MERK to obtain free prescriptions to those who need it.
www.trxaccess.com	• Call (800) 789-8025 to obtain discounts on prescription coverage
www.rocheusa.com	• For patients using Roche products, call (877) 757-6243 for further information on the patient assistance program.
www.myrxadvocate.com	• To receive an application or verify if you qualify, call (877) 331-0362.
	• The address is Select Care Benefits Network, PO Box 500148, Austin, TX 78750.
	• The fax number is (512) 996-9409.

These are just a few of the programs available to ease the burden of paying high costs of prescription medicine. Each program has different rules, guidelines, and so forth.

The National Association of Counties also offers a medical discount card. There is no enrollment or fee to receive this card. It can be used to receive an average discount of 20 percent off prescriptions. Anyone without insurance can use this card. If a person has health insurance but their plan does not cover a specific medication, this card can be used to offset the cost of the medication. In order to be eligible, your county must participate in the program. If you are unsure about your county's status, visit www.naco.org. Once you are at that page, find your county inside your state. In many counties, the cards are available in the county courthouse, local libraries, or town halls.

Gasoline Prices

The price of gas often fluctuates, but there are ways to help alleviate some of the expenses. Some supermarkets offer discounts on gasoline when purchasing groceries. If a local store offers this discount, it might be wise to take advantage of the promotion. During the week of August 23, 2006, gasoline in our area was $2.73 per gallon. The discount from my bonus card entitled us to a discount of $2.43 a gallon. If no grocery stores participate with this incentive in the area, visit www.gasbuddy.com to find the best price on gasoline. After finding your state, you can see who has the least expensive gas in the area. This Web site will provide additional Web sites to help locate the lowest gas station prices locally.

Some Entertainment Books do offer coupons for $1.00 off gas purchases at specific gas stations. The following are some other ways to help alleviate the cost on gasoline:

- Check the air pressure in the tires. If the tires are too low, it will reduce the efficiency of the fuel.

- Driving with the windows down will reduce fuel efficiency. It is much better to use the ventilation system.

- For most cars, it is unnecessary to use a high-octane gasoline, unless specified by the car manufacturer, which can be verified in the owner's manual. Many people believe the octane has to do with the quality of the gasoline, but the octane level only measures how hard it is to ignite the gasoline. Most cars need the octane level of approximately eighty-seven. The high-performance sports car or turbo-charged car utilize the higher levels of octane. If an engine pings or knocks, you may need to use the next higher level.

- Purchase gas when the temperature is at its coolest. If it is a warm season, try to fill the car in the early morning or later in the day. Gas pumps will only measure the volume, not the density. If an individual is in a state where they are permitted to pump their own gas, tip the gas nozzle when finished fueling to get an extra one-third cup of fuel into the tank. Remember to tighten the gas cap because gas can easily evaporate from the tank.

- Remove excessive weight from the trunk. Having approximately 250 pounds in the trunk can result in a reduction of one mile per gallon.

- If the gas mileage drops, check to see if you need a tune-up. The car will burn less gasoline if it is operating well.

- Check the air filter. A dirty air filter may also result in low gas mileage. If you change your own oil, check the air filter when you change your oil.

Income and Business Assistance

If someone is starting a business and needs help writing a business plan, find the local organization of SCORE. This is nonprofit agency will, at no cost, help and advise people in starting their own business.

Web site	Description
www.score.org	• Helps you prepare a business plan
www.sba.gov	• Obtains free information from the Small Business Administration

Online Merchandise

Most of the following Web sites are free, but a couple may require a fee to enroll.

Address	Description
www.amazon.com	• Purchase a vast variety of new and used items
www.sellstufflocal.com	• Provides free classifieds
www.livedeal.com	• Provides free, local classifieds
www.auctions.yahoo.com	• Provides free auctions

www.auctionfire.com	• Provides free auctions
www.webclassifieds.us	• Provides free classifieds
www.buysellcommunity.com	• Free auction site to buy and sell stuff
www.sell.com	• Provides online auctions
www.freedayauctions.com	• Provides online auctions
www.half.com	• Purchase and sell books, music, movies, video games, and game systems
www.ebay.com	• Provides online auctions

These are just a few sites to visit to see what can be listed for sale or purchased. Some sell both new and used products. If a child no longer wants his or her video games, books, and so forth, sell them. If a VCR was replaced with a DVD player, sell the videotapes and replace them with DVDs. The Web sites can provide ideas for items that can be sold.

Crafts

To earn an extra income, assemble some crafts to sell at local craft shows. Rent a table at a flea market and sell some crafts at a garage sale. It is also a nice gesture to make crafts and give them during the holiday season. Visit the following sites to get free craft items and instructions:

Web site	Description
www.craftown.com	• Offers free crafts, including needlepoint, patterns and much more
www.craftfreebies.com	• Offers free patterns, outdoor plans, woodworking plans, and more
	• Provides auctions
www.northpolechristmas.com-	• Offers free Christmas patterns with complete instructions
www.allcrafts.net	• Offers hundreds of free projects available
www.myfree.com	• Offers free books, patterns, and paint brushes
www.creativekidsathome.com	• Offers free craft ideas

www.wwvisions.com	• Offers free projects utilizing items around the home

Web Pages

Web site	Description
www.bravenet.com	• Offers free Web pages
www.freewebs.com	• Offers free Web pages
www.freewebtemplates.com	• Offers free Web site templates

Home and Garden Help

Address	Description
www.landscaping.about.com	• Offers free designs, ideas, and pictures to assist with improving landscaping • Provides links to other helpful websites that relate to landscaping
www.bhg.com	• Offers improvements, ideas, recipes, and more
www.the-landscape-design-site.com	• Provides free professional landscaping advice
www.greatlandscapingideas.com	• Offers free articles to view • Provides free designs for patios, decks, pool landscaping, gardens, and much more

If you want to save money on spring water, this savings is only beneficial for communities who live near filling stations for spring water. An empty one-gallon container will cost $0.25 to refill. People with water coolers can fill an empty five-gallon water container for $1.00.

Chapter Seven:
Let the Savings Begin!

In an effort to make this book as thorough as possible, we have tried to cover all the methods and information to develop the reader into a more efficient shopper. This book provided information covering several topics:

- Obtaining and organizing coupons

- Purchasing multiple items to save money

- Getting the most out of coupons

- Using supermarkets when the face value of the coupons is doubled or tripled

- Developing an educated consumer who can recognize price gimmicks

- Enabling the consumer to comprehend how to purchase some brand-name products for less than store-brand price

- Exchanging unwanted coupons for desired coupons

- Making consumers aware of the various promotions to receive items at little or no cost

- Achieving substantial savings for a vacation

- Saving money using vendor rebates, manufacturer's rebates, "try me free" offers, and rain checks

- Saving money on children's activities, senior programs, college expenses, and help for the disabled

- Saving money on housing and automobiles

- Saving incentives to put money back in your pocket

- Listing a multitude of programs, Web sites, and creative ideas for saving money

As an additional perk for purchasing our book, we request the reader e-mail us at cutitoutbook@aol.com. Please supply us with your first name, the city and state in which you reside, and where you purchased our book. This will enable us to add the reader to our exclusive customer e-mail list. The information we receive will remain private. In the subject section of the e-mail, please type "start saving." In return, we will send additional cost-saving resources as they are acquired. This e-mail address can also be used to obtain an answer to any questions pertaining to the information in our book.

978-0-595-40867-2
0-595-40867-2